SONGS AND RHYMES FOR THE TEACHING O

JULIAN DAKIN

Illustrated by Barbara Lang

Longman

ADDISON WESLEY LONGMAN LIMITED
Edinburgh Gate, Harlow,
Essex CM20 2JE, England
and Associated Companies throughout the world.

This edition first published 1968
Seventy-fourth impression 1997

Produced through Longman Malaysia, TCP

ISBN 0-582-52129-7

FOREWORD

There is a Teacher's Book to accompany this collection of songs and rhymes. It contains a general introduction describing the purpose of this collection and the role of songs and rhymes in language teaching. It also contains tables of rhymes which can be used for practising particular difficulties of pronunciation, vocabulary, and structure. There is a section on how to present the songs and rhymes to children, which also contains many of the tunes and fingerplays traditionally associated with the rhymes. Where a rhyme is marked in this collection with an asterisk* there is a note about it in the Teacher's Book. Where a rhyme is marked with a letter of the alphabet, this indicates the rhythmic shape of the rhyme. There is a full description of rhythmic shapes in the Teacher's Book.

ACKNOWLEDGEMENTS

We are grateful to the following for permission to reproduce copyright material:
A. & C. Black Ltd. for 'Moo Cow Moo Cow' and 'I Like to Skip' by W. Kingdon Ward and 'Swing Me Over the Water' and 'Stir the Soup in the Pot' by Ruth Large from *Speech Rhymes* edited by Clive Sansom, 'Here We Come Galloping', 'Three Little Ponies', 'Tick Tock' (slightly adapted) and 'We Are Indians' by Hilda M. Adams from *Jingle Jangle*; Boosey & Hawkes Music Publishers Ltd. for 'Can You Tell Me What Little Boys Do?' from *Thirty Songs for the Nursery School* by Winnifred E. Houghton, Copyright 1943 by Boosey & Co. Ltd.; Campbell Connelly & Co. Ltd, for 'Hokey Cokey'; The Clarendon Press for 'I did, I did, I did, I did' and 'Polly Ann' from *Speaking and Moving Book I* by Francis Wilkins; J. Curwen & Sons Ltd. for 'Horses, Horses, I Have Got Horses' by C. K. Offer, 'This Old Man', 'Rio Grande' and 'The Animals Went in Two by Two'; Methuen & Co. Ltd. for 'The King's Breakfast' from *When We Were Very Young* by A. A. Milne; Sir Isaac Pitman & Sons Ltd. for 'If Only I Had Plenty of Money' by Paul Edmonds and 'What Are You Going To Be' from *Songs and Marching Tunes for Children*, and 'One Red Engine Puffing Down the Track' and 'Here you can see the Deep Blue Sea' from *Number Rhymes and Finger Plays* by E. R. Boyce and Katherine Bartlett; The Society of Authors as the Literary Representatives of the Estate of the late Rose Fyleman for 'Well I Never, Did You Ever' by Rose Fyleman; Mrs Annick Zandar for 'The Tunes of Lavender's Blue', 'In a wood there grew a tree' and 'Ten green speckled frogs' and United Music Publishers Ltd. on behalf of the publishers/proprietors, S.D.M. of Paris, for 'Brother Peter' from *48 Rondes Enfantines*.

CONTENTS

A*

1* One, Two, Put on Your Shoe (G)
One, two,
Put on your shoe.
Three four,
Shut the door.
Five, six,
Pick up sticks.
Seven, eight,
Eat off a plate.
Nine, ten,
Say it again.

2* One, Two, Three, Play With Me (B)
One, two, three,
Play with me.
Four, five, six,
Pick up sticks.
Seven, eight, nine,
Walk in line.

3* What Does The Cat Say
What does the cat say? Meow, Meow.
What does the dog say? Bow Wow.
What does the donkey say? Ee Aw.
What does the crow say? Caw, Caw.
What does the farmer say? Shoo, Shoo.
What does the cow say? Moo, Moo.
What do they all say?

4* One Man Went To Mow (B)
One man went to mow,
Went to mow a meadow,
One man and his dog,
Went to mow a meadow.

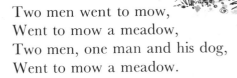

Two men went to mow,
Went to mow a meadow,
Two men, one man and his dog,
Went to mow a meadow.

Three men went to mow, etc.

5* Head And Shoulders, Knees And Toes (A)

Head and shoulders, knees and toes,
   knees and toes,
Head and shoulders, knees and toes,
   knees and toes,
And eyes, and ears, and mouth, and nose,
Head and shoulders, knees and toes,
   knees and toes.

6 One Red Engine (A)

One red engine puffing down the track,
One red engine puffing back.
Two red engines puffing down the track, etc.

7* This Is The Great Big Indian Chief (F)

This is the great big Indian Chief.
This is his arrow and his bow.
This is his wigwam.
This is his flute,
And this is the way he sits, just so.

8* Moo Cow, Moo Cow (G)

Moo cow, moo cow,
How do you do, cow?
Very well, thank you,
Moo, moo, moo.

9* Sammy Thumb (G)

Sammy Thumb, Sammy Thumb,
Where are you?
Here I am! Here I am!
How do you do!

Peter Pointer, Peter Pointer,
Where are you?
Here I am! Here I am!
How do you do!

Bobby Big, Bobby Big,
Where are you?
Here I am! Here I am!
How do you do!

Ruby Ring, Ruby Ring,
Where are you?
Here I am! Here I am!
How do you do!

Tiny Tim, Tiny Tim,
Where are you?
Here I am! Here I am!
How do you do!

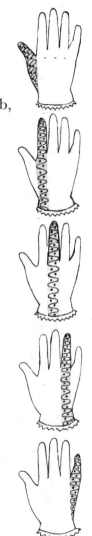

10* **Where Is Thumbkin** (G)

Where is Thumbkin?
Where is Thumbkin?
Here I am,
Here I am.
How are you today, sir?
Very well, thank you.
Run away.

Where is Pointer?
Where is Pointer?
Here I am,
Here I am.
How are you today, sir?
Very well, thank you.
Run away.

Where is Bigman?
Where is Bigman?
Here I am,
Here I am.
How are you today, sir?
Very well, thank you.
Run away.

Where is Ringman?
Where is Ringman?
Here I am,
Here I am.
How are you today, sir?
Very well, thank you.
Run away.

Where is Pinkie?
Where is Pinkie?
Here I am,
Here I am.
How are you today, sir?
Very well, thank you.
Run away.

11* **Polly Put The Kettle On**

Polly, put the kettle on,
Polly, put the kettle on,
Polly, put the kettle on,
We'll all have some tea.

Sukie, take it off again,
Sukie, take it off again,
Sukie, take it off again,
We're all going away.

12* I've Got Ten Little Fingers

I've got ten little fingers.
I've got ten little toes.
I've got two ears,
I've got two eyes,
And just one little nose.

13 Farmer Brown's Got One Big Dog (C)

Farmer Brown's got one big dog,
Bow, wow, wow, wow, wow.
One big dog and two small puppies,
Bow, wow, wow, wow, wow.

Farmer Brown's got three big cats,
Meow, meow, meow, meow, meow.
Three big cats and four small kittens,
Meow, meow, meow, meow, meow.

Farmer Brown's got five big cows,
Moo, moo, moo, moo, moo.
Five big cows and six small calves,
Moo, moo, moo, moo, moo.

Farmer Brown's got seven big ducks,
Quack, quack, quack, quack, quack.
Seven big ducks and eight small ducklings,
Quack, quack, quack, quack, quack.

Farmer Brown's got nine big sheep,
Ba, ba, ba, ba, ba.
Nine big sheep and ten small lambs,
Ba, ba, ba, ba, ba.

14* This Is The Way (A)

This is the way we wash our face,
Wash our face, wash our face,
This is the way we wash our face,
At seven o'clock in the morning.

This is the way we clean our teeth,
Clean our teeth, clean our teeth,
This is the way we clean our teeth,
At seven o'clock in the morning.

This is the way we comb our hair,
Comb our hair, comb our hair,
This is the way we comb our hair,
At seven o'clock in the morning.

This is the way we eat our breakfast,
Eat our breakfast, eat our breakfast,
This is the way we eat our breakfast,
At eight o'clock in the morning.

This is the way we wash the dishes,
Wash the dishes, wash the dishes,
This is the way we wash the dishes,
At nine o'clock in the morning.

This is the way we sweep the floor,
Sweep the floor, sweep the floor,
This is the way we sweep the floor,
At ten o'clock in the morning.

This is the way we drink our milk,
Drink our milk, drink our milk,
This is the way we drink our milk,
At eleven o'clock in the morning.

This is the way we cook our dinner,
Cook our dinner, cook our dinner,
This is the way we cook our dinner,
At twelve o'clock in the morning.

This is the way we go to bed,
Go to bed, go to bed,
This is the way we go to bed,
At ten o'clock in the evening.

15* X Is Wearing A Bright Blue Dress
X is wearing a bright blue dress,
Bright blue dress, bright blue dress,
X is wearing a bright blue dress,
All day long.

Y is wearing a bright green shirt,
Bright green shirt, bright green shirt,
Y is wearing a bright green shirt,
All day long.

A**

16 One Little Girl (A)
One little girl sat on the ground,
One little girl danced round and round,
One little girl danced here, danced there,
One little girl danced everywhere.

Two little girls sat on the ground, etc.

17* Rain, Rain, Go Away (A)
Rain, rain, go away,
This is mother's washing day,
Come again, another day.

18* Two Little Birds Sitting On A Wall (G)
Two little birds
Sitting on a wall,
One called Peter,
One called Paul.

Fly away Peter,
Fly away Paul,
Come back Peter,
Come back Paul.

19* I Like To Skip (I)

I like to skip,
I like to jump,
I like to run about,
I like to play,
I like to sing,
I like to laugh and shout.

20* The Farmer's In His House (G)

The farmer's in his house
The farmer's in his house
E, I, E, I,
The farmer's in his house.

The farmer wants a wife, etc.
The wife wants a son, etc.
The son wants a dog, etc.
The dog wants a bone, etc.
We all bring the bone, etc.

21* Two Clean Hands And Two Big Thumbs

Two clean hands and two big thumbs.
Eight little fingers, ten little toes
One round head going nod, nod, nodding.
Two eyes peeping, one small nose.

22* Old Macdonald Had A Farm (C)

Old Macdonald had a farm,
E, I, E, I, O,
And on that farm he had some ducks,
E, I, E, I, O,
With a quack quack here and a quack, quack
    there,
Here a quack, there a quack,
Everywhere a quack, quack.
Old Macdonald had a farm,
E, I, E, I, O.

Old Macdonald had a farm,
E, I, E, I, O,
And on that farm he had some cows,
E, I, E, I, O,
With a moo-moo here, etc.

23* Brother Peter (G)

Brother Peter,
Brother Peter,
Sleeps too well,
Sleeps too well,
Ring the bell for breakfast,
Ring the bell for breakfast,
Ding dong bell,
Ding dong bell.

24* Hickory, Dickory, Dock (F)

Hickory, dickory, dock.
The mouse ran up the clock.
The clock struck one,
The mouse ran down,
Hickory, dickory, dock.

25 Diddle, Diddle, Dumpling (A)

Diddle, diddle, dumpling, my son John,
Went to bed with his trousers on.
One shoe off and one shoe on,
Diddle, diddle dumpling, my son John.

26* Can You Tell Me

Can you tell me,
Can you tell me,
What little boys do?
They run and jump.
They run and jump,
So I will jump too.

Can you tell me,
Can you tell me,
What little girls do?
They dance and skip,
They dance and skip,
So I will skip too.

Can you tell me,
Can you tell me,
What little soldiers do?
They fight and march,
They fight and march,
So I will march too.

Can you tell me,
Can you tell me,
What little people do?
They play and work,
They play and work,
So I will work too.

Can you tell me,
Can you tell me,
What little babies do?
They eat and sleep,
They eat and sleep,
So I will sleep too.

27* London's Burning (G)
London's burning,
London's burning,
Fetch the engines,
Fetch the engines,
Fire, fire,
Fire, fire,
Pour on water,
Pour on water.

28* I Did, I Did, I Did (B)
I did, I did, I did
I did my washing today
I did my washing today
And now it's time to play.

I did, I did, I did
I did my work today
I did my work today
And now it's time to play.

When I was a grocer,
A grocer, a grocer,
When I was a grocer,
This was how I went.

When I was a farmer,
A farmer, a farmer,
When I was a farmer,
This was how I went.

When I was a carpenter,
A carpenter, a carpenter,
When I was a carpenter,
This was how I went.

When I was a fisherman,
A fisherman, a fisherman,
When I was a fisherman,
This was how I went.

30* **Ladybird, Ladybird** **(G)**
Ladybird, ladybird,
Fly away home,
Your house is on fire,
Your children all gone.

29* **When I Was A Soldier** **(G)**
When I was a soldier,
A soldier, a soldier,
When I was a soldier,
This was how I went.

When I was a policeman,
A policeman, a policeman,
When I was a policeman,
This was how I went.

31 Fish, Fish, All In A Dish (A)

Fish, fish, all in a dish
Who will eat my beautiful fish?
Fish, fish, all in a dish.

32* This Little Pig. (B)

This little pig went to market,
This little pig stayed at home,
This little pig had roast beef,
This little pig had none,
And this little pig went wee, wee, wee,
All the way home.

33* What Are You Going To Be (B)

What are you going to be?
What are you going to be?
I shall be a soldier
That's the life for me.

What are you going to be?
What are you going to be?
I shall be a garage hand,
That's the life for me.

What are you going to be?
What are you going to be?
I shall be a fireman,
That's the life for me.

34 Swing Me (B)

Swing me over the water,
Swing me over the sea,
Swing me over the garden wall,
And swing me home for tea.

35* Cobbler, Cobbler, Mend My Shoe (A)

Cobbler, cobbler, mend my shoe,
Have it ready by half past two,
Come along and get your shoe
It's ready now, it's half past two.

36* Abracadabra

Abracadabra, wizzy woo,
I can fly and so can you.

37* Hot Cross Buns (G)

Hot cross buns,
Hot cross buns,
One a penny, two a penny,
Hot cross buns.

If you have no daughters,
Give them to your sons,
One a penny, two a penny,
Hot cross buns.

38* We Have Come For Polly Ann (D)

We have come for Polly Ann,
Polly Ann, Polly Ann,
We have come for Polly Ann
Can she come out to play?
Polly Ann is sweeping,
Polly Ann is sweeping,
Polly Ann is sweeping,
She can't come out to play.

We have come for Polly Ann,
Polly Ann, Polly Ann,
We have come for Polly Ann,
Can she come out to play?
Polly Ann is eating,
Polly Ann is eating,
Polly Ann is eating,
She can't come out to play.

39* This Old Man (F)

This old man, he played one,
He played knick knack on my thumb,
With a knick knack paddy wack
Give a dog a bone,
This old man came rolling home.

This old man, he played two,
He played knick knack on my shoe, etc.

This old man, he played three,
He played knick knack on my knee, etc.

This old man, he played four,
He played knick knack on my door, etc.

This old man, he played five,
He played knick knack on my hive, etc.

This old man, he played six,
He played knick knack on my sticks, etc.

This old man, he played seven,
He played knick knack up in heaven, etc.

This old man, he played eight,
He played knick knack on my gate, etc.

This old man, he played nine,
He played knick knack in a line, etc.

This old man, he played ten,
He played knick knack once again, etc.

40* One, Two, Three, Four (A)

One, two, three, four,
Come in please and shut the door.
Five, six, seven, eight,
It's time for school. You're very late.
Nine, ten, nine, ten,
Don't be late for school again.

41* One, Two, Three, Four, Five (A)

One, two, three, four, five,
Once I caught a fish alive,
Six, seven, eight, nine, ten,
Then I let it go again.
Why did you let it go?
Because it bit my finger so.
Which finger did it bite?
The little finger on the right.

42* Baa, Baa, Black Sheep (G)

Baa, baa, black sheep,
Have you any wool?
Yes sir, yes sir,
Three bags full.
One for the master,
One for the dame,
And one for the little boy
Who lives down the lane.

43* Ten Little Squirrels (A)

Ten little squirrels sitting in a tree
The first two said:
  What can we see?
The next two said:
  A man with a gun.
The next two said:
  Let's run. Let's run.
The next two said:
  Let's hide in the shade.
The last two said:
  We're not afraid!
But BANG went the gun and away they all ran.

A***

44* Rat A Tat Tat

Rat a tat, tat,
Who is that?
Only Grandma's Pussy cat.
What do you want?
A bottle of milk.
Where is your money?
In my pocket.
Where is your pocket?
I forgot it.
Oh you silly Pussy cat!

45* A, B, C, D, E, F, G (A)

A, B, C, D, E, F, G,
John is hiding far from me.
Looking here, looking there,
I can't see him anywhere.
Pitter pat. What is that?
Oh, it's just a pussy cat.

48* **One Busy Housewife** **(A)**
One busy housewife sweeping up the floor,
Two busy housewives polishing the door,
Three busy housewives washing all the socks,
Four busy housewives winding up the clocks,
Five busy housewives cleaning with the broom,
Six busy housewives tidying the room,
Seven busy housewives washing in the sink,
Eight busy housewives giving the cat a drink.
Nine busy housewives cooking dinner too,
Ten busy housewives with nothing left to do.

46 **Little Jack Sprat** **(G)**
Little Jack Sprat,
Once had a pig.
It was not very little,
It was not very big.

It was not very thin,
It was not very fat,
"It's a good pig to eat",
Said little Jack Sprat.

47* **Hokey Cokey**
You put your right foot in,
You take your right foot out,
You put your right foot in,
And you shake it all about.
You do the Hokey Cokey
And you turn around,
That's what it's all about.
Oh Hokey Cokey,
Oh Hokey Cokey,
Oh Hokey Cokey.
That's what it's all about.

You put your right hand in, et

49* **Blue Is The Sea** **(G)**

Blue is the sea,
Green is the grass,
White are the clouds,
As they slowly pass.
Black are the crows,
Brown the trees,
Red are the sails,
Of a ship in the breeze.

There were nine in the bed, etc.

There were two in the bed,
And the little one said,
Roll over,
Roll over.
So they both rolled over,
And one fell out.

There was one in the bed,
And the little one said,
Roll over,
Roll over.
So he rolled over,
And he fell out.

50* **There Were Ten In The Bed** **(G)**

There were ten in the bed,
And the little one said,
Roll over,
Roll over.
So they all rolled over,
And one fell out.

There were none in the bed,
And no one said,
Roll over,
Roll over.
So no one rolled over,
And no one fell out.

51* Three Blind Mice
Three blind mice,
Three blind mice.
See how they run,
See how they run.
They all ran after the farmer's wife,
Who cut off their tails with a carving knife.
Did you ever see such a sight in your life,
As three blind mice?

52* Here Is A Church (G)
Here is a church
And here the steeple,
Open the door
And out come the people.
Here is the minister
Going upstairs
Here is the minister
Saying his prayers.

53 Stir The Soup
Stir the soup in the pot,
Make it nice and hot,
Round and round and round and round,
Stir the soup in the pot.

54 Insey Winsey Spider (B)
Insey Winsey Spider
Climbing up the spout,
Down came the rain and
Washed the spider out.
Out came the sun and
Dried up all the rain.
Insey Winsey Spider,
Climbing up again.

55 Mary Ann, Mary Ann (A)
Mary Ann, Mary Ann,
Make the porridge in a pan.
Make it thick, make it thin,
Make it any way you can.

56   Pat A Cake   (A)

Pat a cake, pat a cake, baker's man,
Bake me a cake as fast as you can.
Pat it and prick it and mark it with "B"
Put it in the oven for baby and me.

57*   Solomon Grundy   (G)

Solomon Grundy,
Born on Monday,
Christened on Tuesday,
Married on Wednesday,
Sick on Thursday,
Worse on Friday,
Died on Saturday,
Buried on Sunday.

58   Pussy Cat, Pussy Cat   (H)

Pussy cat, Pussy cat,
Where have you been?
I've been to London to see the Queen.
Pussy cat, Pussy cat,
What did you do there?
I frightened a little mouse under the chair.

59   Georgie Porgie   (A)

Georgie Porgie, pudding and pie,
Kissed the girls and made them cry.
When the boys came out to play,
Georgie Porgie ran away!

60   Humpty Dumpty   (F)

Humpty Dumpty sat on a wall.
Humpty Dumpty had a great fall.
All the king's horses
And all the king's men
Couldn't put Humpty together again.

61* **On My Blackboard I Can Draw** **(A)**
On my blackboard I can draw
One little house with one green door,
Two brown gates that open wide,
Three red steps that lead inside,
Four little chimneys painted white,
Five little windows shining bright,
Six yellow daffodils straight and tall,
Growing up against the wall.

62 **Flying Man** **(G)**
Flying man, Flying man,
Up in the sky,
Where are you going to
Flying so high?
Over the mountains
And over the sea,
Flying man, Flying man
Won't you take me?

63* **Ride A Cock Horse** **(A)**
Ride a cock horse to Banbury Cross,
See a fine lady on a white horse,
Rings on her fingers and bells on her toes,
She shall have music wherever she goes.

64* **Here You Can See The Deep Blue Sea** **(A)**
Here you can see the deep blue sea,
This is the boat and this is me,
All the little fishes down below,
Waggle their tails and off they go.

65 **Jack and Jill** **(C)**
Jack and Jill went up the hill
To fetch a pail of water.
Jack fell down and broke his crown
And Jill came tumbling after.

68 Tick Tock (G)
Tick Tock
Goes the clock,
Telling the time
All by itself.
Round and round
The two hands go,
The big one quickly,
The little one slow.

69* Where Are You Going, My Little Cat?
Where are you going, my little cat?
I'm going to town to buy a new hat.
What? A hat for a cat? A cat to buy a hat?
Your head is too round, and your face is too flat
To wear a hat.
Who ever heard of a cat with a hat?

66 We Are Indians (G)
We are Indians,
Creeping through the jungle
On silent foot.
Looking for animals,
Hunting for animals,
Searching for animals,
And ready to shoot.

67 Five Little Firemen (A)
Five little firemen standing in a row,
One, two, three, four, five, they go.
Off went the engine with a shout,
Quicker than a wink the fire was out.

70* White Sheep, White Sheep (G)
White sheep, white sheep,
On a blue hill,
When the wind stops
You all stand still.
You all run away,
When the winds blow.
White sheep, white sheep,
Where do you go?

71 Hey Diddle, Diddle (C)
Hey diddle, diddle, the cat and the fiddle,
The cow jumped over the moon.
The little dog laughed to see such fun,
And the dish ran away with the spoon.

72 Little Miss Muffet (I)
Little Miss Muffet
Sat on a tuffet,
Eating her curds and whey.
There came a big spider
Who sat down beside her
And frightened Miss Muffet away.

73 Little Jack Horner (I)
Little Jack Horner
Sat in the corner,
Eating a Christmas pie.
He put in his thumb
And pulled out a plum
And said what a good boy am I!

74 Wee Willie Winkie (A)
Wee Willie Winkie runs through the town,
Upstairs, downstairs in his nightgown,
Knocking at the window, crying through the
        lock,
"Are the children in their beds, for now it's
        eight o'clock?"

75* Every Morning At Eight O'clock (A)
Every morning at eight o'clock
You can hear the postman knock.
Up jumps Mary to open the door,
One letter, two letters, three letters, four.

76* **Tinker, Tailor**
Tinker, tailor, soldier, sailor,
Rich man, poor man, beggar man, thief.

77* **Silk, Satin**
Silk, satin, cotton, rags.

78* **This Year, Next Year**
This year, next year,
Sometime, never.

79* **One Potato, Two Potatoes**   **(G)**
One potato, two potatoes,
Three potatoes, four,
Five potatoes, six potatoes,
Seven potatoes, more.

O U T, spells out,
So out you must go
Because the king
And queen say so.

80* **Ten Green Bottles**   **(A)**
Ten green bottles standing on the wall,
Ten green bottles standing on the wall,
And if one green bottle should accidentally fall,
There'd be nine green bottles standing on the
   wall.

Nine green bottles standing on the wall, etc.

81* **A Train Going Up A Hill**   **(G)**
I wish I could,
I wish I could,
I wish I could.

I think I can,
I think I can,
I think I can.

I thought I could,
I thought I could,
I thought I could.

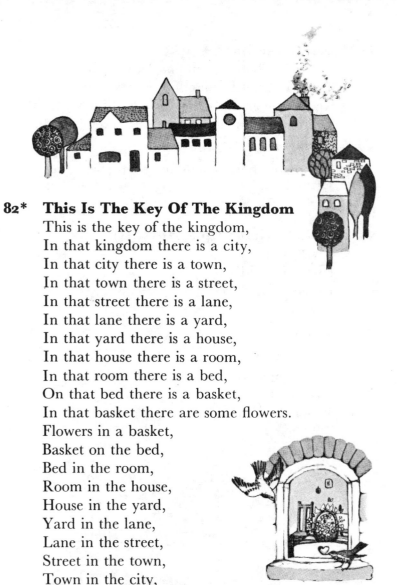

82* This Is The Key Of The Kingdom
This is the key of the kingdom,
In that kingdom there is a city,
In that city there is a town,
In that town there is a street,
In that street there is a lane,
In that lane there is a yard,
In that yard there is a house,
In that house there is a room,
In that room there is a bed,
On that bed there is a basket,
In that basket there are some flowers.
Flowers in a basket,
Basket on the bed,
Bed in the room,
Room in the house,
House in the yard,
Yard in the lane,
Lane in the street,
Street in the town,
Town in the city,
City in the kingdom.
Of that kingdom this is the key.

83* Eeny, Meeny, Miny, Mo (A)
Eeny, meeny, miny, mo,
Catch a monkey by his toe,
If he hollers, let him go,
Eeny, meeny, miny, mo.

84 There Was A Little Girl (I)
There was a little girl,
Who had a little curl
Right in the middle of her forehead.
And when she was good,
She was very, very, good,
But when she was bad, she was horrid.

85 It's Raining, It's Pouring (F)
It's raining, it's pouring.
The old man is snoring.
He jumped into bed
And bumped his head
And couldn't get up in the morning.

86 Here We Come Galloping (C)
Here we come galloping, galloping, galloping,
Galloping over the down,
Robin is riding a dapple grey pony,
My little pony is brown.

87 Three Little Ponies (A)
Three little ponies are trotting into town,
One black, one white, and one of them brown.

88 I Hear Thunder (G)
I hear thunder,
I hear thunder,
Hark, don't you?
Hark, don't you?
Patter go the raindrops,
Patter go the raindrops,
I'm wet through,
I'm wet through.

89* Fee, Fie, Foe, Fum
Fee, fie, foe, fum,
I smell the blood of an Englishman.

90* The Brave Old Duke Of York (E)
Oh, the brave old duke of York,
He had ten thousand men,
He marched them up to the top of the hill,
And he marched them down again.
And when they were up, they were up,
And when they were down, they were down,
And when they were only half-way up
They were neither up nor down.

93   Did You Ever?   (G)
Well, I never!
Did you ever
See a monkey
Dressed in leather?

94*   John Brown's Baby   (D)
John Brown's baby's got a cold upon his chest,
John Brown's baby's got a cold upon his chest,
John Brown's baby's got a cold upon his chest,
But we all go marching on.
Glory, glory, hallelujah,
Glory, glory, hallelujah,
Glory, glory, hallelujah,
But we all go marching on.

91*   As I Was Going To St. Ives   (A)
As I was going to St. Ives,
I met a man with seven wives.
Every wife had seven sacks.
Every sack had seven cats.
Every cat had seven kittens.
Kittens, cats, sacks and wives,
How many were there going to St. Ives?

95   Horses, Horses
Horses, horses, I've got horses,
White and dapple grey.
When I give them corn to eat,
They jump five and twenty feet.

92*   I Went Up A Pair Of Stairs
I went up a pair of stairs. Just like me.
I went up two pairs of stairs. Just like me.
I went into a room. Just like me.
I looked out of the window. Just like me.
And there I saw a monkey. Just like me.

96* There's A Hole In My Bucket

There's a hole in my bucket,
Dear Liza, dear Liza,
There's a hole in my bucket,
Oh, what shall I do?

Why, mend it, dear Henry,
Dear Henry, dear Henry,
Why, mend it, dear Henry,
Dear Henry, mend it.

With what shall I mend it?
Dear Liza, dear Liza,
With what shall I mend it?
Oh, what shall I do?

With sticky, dear Henry,
Dear Henry, dear Henry,
With sticky, dear Henry,
Dear Henry, with sticky.

But there isn't any sticky,
Dear Liza, dear Liza,
But there isn't any sticky,
Oh, what shall I do?

Well, make some, dear Henry,
Dear Henry, dear Henry,
Well, make some, dear Henry.
Dear Henry, make some.

With what shall I make it?
Dear Liza, dear Liza,
With what shall I make it?
Oh, what shall I do?

With powder and water,
Dear Henry, dear Henry,
With powder and water,
Both mixed together.

But there isn't any water,
Dear Liza, dear Liza,
But there isn't any water,
Oh, what shall I do?

Well, fetch some, dear Henry,
Dear Henry, dear Henry,
Well, fetch some, dear Henry,
Dear Henry, fetch some.

In what shall I fetch it?
Dear Liza, dear Liza,
In what shall I fetch it?
Oh, what shall I do?

In a bucket, dear Henry,
Dear Henry, dear Henry,
In a bucket, dear Henry,
Dear Henry, in a bucket.

But there's a hole in my bucket,
Dear Liza, dear Liza,
There's a hole in my bucket,
Oh, what *shall* I do!

97*   Ten Little Indians   (A)

Ten little Indians standing in a line,
One went home and then there were nine.

Nine little Indians, sitting on a gate,
One fell off and then there were eight.

Eight little Indians, looking up at heaven,
One fell down and then there were seven.

Seven little Indians playing with sticks,
One broke his head and then there were six.

Six little Indians playing with knives,
One was killed and then there were five.

Five little Indians pushing at the door,
One fell in and then there were four.

Four little Indians sitting in a tree,
One fell down and then there were three.

Three little Indians, out in a canoe,
One fell overboard, and then there were two.

Two little Indians playing with a gun,
One shot the other, and then there was one.

One little Indian with his little wife,
Lived in a wigwam the rest of his life.

One daddy Indian, one mummy squaw,
Soon had a family of ten Indians more.

98*   Miss Polly Had A Dolly   (A)

Miss Polly had a dolly who was sick, sick, sick,
And she phoned for the doctor to come quick,
   quick, quick.
The doctor came with his bag and his hat
And he knocked at the door with a rat tat tat.
He looked at the dolly and he shook his head,
And he said, "Miss Polly, you must put her
   straight to bed.
Wrap her up warm, and keep her very still,
I'll be back in the morning with my bill, bill,
   bill."

**99   There Was An Old Woman Who Lived In
A Shoe   (A)**

There was an old woman who lived in a shoe.
She had so many children, she didn't know what
   to do.
She gave them some soup without any bread,
And smacked them all soundly and sent them
   to bed.

100   There Was A Crooked Man (A)

There was a crooked man and he went a
   crooked mile,
He found a crooked sixpence against a crooked
   stile,
He bought a crooked cat which caught a
   crooked mouse,
And they all lived together in a little crooked
   house.

101*   The Farmer Sows His Seeds (E)

The farmer sows his seeds,
The farmer sows his seeds,
Oats, beans and barley O
The farmer sows his seeds.

The wind begins to blow,
The wind begins to blow,
Oats, beans and barley O
The wind begins to blow.

The rain begins to fall,
The rain begins to fall,
Oats, beans and barley O
The rain begins to fall.

The sun begins to shine,
The sun begins to shine,
Oats, beans and barley O
The sun begins to shine.

The wheat begins to grow,
The wheat begins to grow,
Oats, beans and barley O
The wheat begins to grow.

The farmer cuts the grain,
The farmer cuts the grain,
Oats, beans and barley O
The farmer cuts the grain.

The farmer binds the sheaves,
The farmer binds the sheaves,
Oats, beans and barley O
The farmer binds the sheaves.

And now the harvest's in,
And now the harvest's in,
Oats, beans and barley O
And now the harvest's in.

102* The Little Brown Jug (A)

My wife and I live all alone
In a little brown hut we call our own,
She likes gin and I like rum,
Ha, ha, ha, we have some fun.
Ha, ha, ha, hee, hee, hee,
Little brown jug, just you and me,
Ha, ha, ha, hee, hee, hee,
Little brown jug, just you and me.

103* Hush Little Baby (A)

Hush little baby, don't say a word,
Mummy will give you a mocking bird.

And if that mocking bird won't sing,
Mummy will give you a diamond ring.

And if that diamond ring gets broken,
Mummy will give you a billy goat.

And if that billy goat won't pull,
Mummy will give you a cart and bull.

And if that cart and bull turns over,
Mummy will give you a dog named Rover.

And if that dog named Rover won't bark,
Mummy will give you a horse and cart.

And if that horse and cart breaks down,
You'll still be the sweetest little baby in town.

104 If All The Seas Were One Sea (C)

If all the seas were one sea,
What a great sea it would be!
And if all the trees were one tree,
What a great tree it would be!
And if this tree were to fall in the sea,
My! What a splish-splash there would be!

105* **Lavender's Blue**
Lavender's blue, dilly dilly,
Lavender's green,
When I am king, dilly dilly,
You shall be queen.

106* **Lilies Are White**
Lilies are white, dilly dilly,
Rosemary's green,
When you are king, dilly dilly,
I will be queen.
Roses are red, dilly dilly,
Lavender's blue,
If you have me, dilly dilly,
I will have you.

107* **Little Bo-peep**   **(F)**
Little Bo-peep has lost her sheep
And doesn't know where to find them.
Leave them alone, and they'll come home,
Bringing their tails behind them.

108* **Sing A Song Of Sixpence**   **(C)**
Sing a song of sixpence
A pocket full of rye,
Four and twenty blackbirds
Baked in the pie.
When the pie was opened,
The birds began to sing,
Oh, wasn't that a dainty dish
To put before the king.

The king was in his counting house,
Counting out his money.
The queen was in the parlour,
Eating bread and honey.
The maid was in the garden,
Hanging out the clothes,
When down came a blackbird
And pecked off her nose.

109 Fire, Fire (A)

Fire, fire, said Mrs. Dyer,
Where, where? said Mrs. Dare,
Up the town, said Mrs. Brown,
Any damage? asked Mrs. Gamage,
None at all, said Mrs. Hall.

110 If All The World Were Paper (E)

If all the world were paper,
And all the sea were ink,
And all the trees were bread and cheese,
What should we do for drink?

111* Oh Dear, What Can The Matter Be? (D)

Oh dear, what can the matter be?
Dear, dear, what can the matter be?
Oh dear, what can the matter be?
Johnny's so long at the fair.

He promised to buy me a bunch of blue ribbons,
He promised to buy me a bunch of blue ribbons,
He promised to buy me a bunch of blue ribbons,
To tie up my pretty brown hair.

He promised to buy me a bunch of pink flowers,
He promised to buy me a bunch of pink flowers,
He promised to buy me a bunch of pink flowers,
To put in my pretty brown hair.

112 Little Boy Blue (A)

Little Boy Blue, come blow your horn,
The cow's in the meadow, the sheep's in the
   corn.
Where is the boy that looks after the sheep?
He's under the haystack fast asleep.
Will you wake him? No, not I,
For if I do, he's sure to cry.

113*   The North Wind Does Blow   (H)

The North Wind does blow
And we shall have snow,
And what will the robin do then, poor thing?
He'll sit in a barn,
And keep himself warm,
And hide his head under his wing, poor thing.

The North Wind does blow
And we shall have snow,
And what will the children do then, poor things?
When lessons are done,
They must skip, jump and run
Until they have made themselves warm, poor
   things.

114   Roses Come, Roses Go   (A)

Roses come, roses go,
Violets begin to blow,
Neither you nor I may know
Why they come or why they go.

115   Goosey, Goosey Gander   (C)

Goosey, goosey gander
Where shall I wander?
Upstairs and downstairs
And in my ladies chamber.
There I met an old man
Who wouldn't say his prayers.
I took him by the left leg
And threw him down the stairs.

116*   The Little Nut Tree   (C)

I had a little nut tree
And nothing would it bear,
Except a silver nutmeg
And a golden pear.
The king of Spain's daughter
Came to visit me,
And all for the sake
Of my little nut tree.
I skipped over the water,
I danced over the sea,
And all the birds in the air
Couldn't catch me.

117   If Only I Had Plenty Of Money   (A)

If only I had plenty of money
I'd buy you some flowers and I'd buy you some
   honey.
I'd buy you a boat and I'd buy you a sail,
I'd buy you a cat with a long bushy tail,
I'd buy you a church and I'd buy you a bell,
I'd buy you a brooch and a bangle as well,
I'd buy you the earth, I'd buy you the moon,
Oh, money, dear money, please come very soon.

118*   Rio

I'll sing you a song of the fish of the sea,
Oh Rio,
I'll sing you a song of the fish of the sea,
For we're bound for the Rio Grande.
Then away, love away, way down Rio,
So fare you well, my pretty young girl,
For we're bound for the Rio Grande.

Sing goodbye to Sally and goodbye to Sue,
Oh Rio,
And you who are listening, goodbye to you,
For we're bound for the Rio Grande.
Then away, love away, way down Rio.
So fare you well, my pretty young girl,
For we're bound for the Rio Grande.

119*   I Love Sixpence   (A)

I love sixpence, jolly little sixpence,
I love sixpence, better than my life.
I'll spend a penny of it, and I'll lend a penny of
   it
And I'll take fourpence home to my wife.

I love fourpence, jolly little fourpence,
I love fourpence, better than my life.
I'll spend a penny of it, and I'll lend a penny of
   it
And I'll take twopence home to my wife.

I love twopence, jolly little twopence,
I love twopence better than my life,
I'll spend a penny of it and I'll lend a penny of
   it
And I'll take nothing home to my wife.

I love nothing, jolly little nothing.
What can nothing buy for my wife?
I have nothing to spend and I have nothing
   to lend
And I love nothing better than my life.

120 John, John, John

John, John, John,
Where have you been to be so long?
Down in the alley, kissing Sally,
Picking up cinders, breaking windows,
John, John, John.

121* In A Wood There Grew A Tree (D)

In a wood there grew a tree,
The best tree, you ever did see
And the green leaves grew all around, all
     around,
And the green leaves grew all around.

And on this tree there was a branch,
The best branch you ever did see,
The branch was on the tree,
The tree was in the wood,
And the green leaves grew all around, all
     around,
And the green leaves grew all around.

And on this branch there was a nest,
The best nest you ever did see,
The nest was on the branch,
The branch was on the tree,
The tree was in the wood,
And the green leaves grew all around, all
     around,
And the green leaves grew all around.

And in this nest there was an egg, etc.
And in this egg there was a yolk, etc.
And in this yolk there was a bird, etc.
And on this bird there was a feather, etc.

122* I'm A Brave, Brave Mouse (G)

I'm a brave, brave mouse.
I go marching through the house,
And I'm not afraid of anything.
For danger I'm prepared,
And I'm never, never scared.
No, I'm not afraid of anything.

What about a cat?
What—a cat?
Yes a cat!
Big and fat.
Well, except for a cat—
I'm not afraid of anything.

I'm a brave, brave mouse.
I go marching through the house,
And I'm not afraid of anything.
For danger I'm prepared,
And I'm never, never scared.
No, I'm not afraid of anything.
What about a trap?
What—a trap?
Yes a trap!
That goes snap.
Well, except for a trap—
I'm not afraid of anything.

I'm a brave, brave mouse.
I go marching through the house,
And I'm not afraid of anything.
For danger I'm prepared,
And I'm never, never scared,
No, I'm not afraid of anything.
What about an owl?
What—an owl?
Yes an owl—
On the prowl.
Well, except for an owl—
I'm not afraid of anything.

123* **The House That Jack Built** **(G)**
This is the house that Jack built.
This is the malt, that lay in the house that Jack
  built.
This is the rat, that ate the malt, that lay in the
  house that Jack built.

This is the cat, that killed the rat, that ate the
  malt, that lay in the house that Jack built.

This is the dog, that chased the cat, that killed
  the rat, that ate the malt, that lay in the
  house that Jack built.

This is the cow with the twisted horn, that tossed
  the dog, that chased the cat, that killed the
  rat, that ate the malt, that lay in the house
  that Jack built.

This is the maiden all forlorn, that milked the
cow with the twisted horn, that tossed the
dog, that chased the cat, that killed the rat,
that ate the malt, that lay in the house that
Jack built.

This is the man all tattered and torn, that
kissed the maiden all forlorn, that milked
the cow with the twisted horn, that tossed
the dog, that chased the cat, that killed the
rat, that ate the malt, that lay in the house
that Jack built.

This is the priest, all shaven and shorn, that
married the man all tattered and torn, that
kissed the maiden all forlorn, that milked the
cow with the twisted horn, that tossed the
dog, that chased the cat, that killed the rat,
that ate the malt, that lay in the house that
Jack built.

This is the cock, that crowed in the morn, that
woke the priest all shaven and shorn, that
married the man all tattered and torn, that
kissed the maiden all forlorn, that milked the
cow with the twisted horn, that tossed the
dog, that chased the cat, that killed the rat,
that ate the malt, that lay in the house that
Jack built.

124* **The Animals Went In Two By Two**

The animals went in two by two, hurrah,
   hurrah,
The animals went in two by two, hurrah,
   hurrah.
The animals went in two by two, the elephant
   and the kangaroo,
And they all went into the ark,
Just to get out of the rain.

The animals went in three by three, hurrah,
   hurrah,
The animals went in three by three, hurrah,
   hurrah.
The animals went in three by three, the wasp,
   the ant and the bumble bee,
And they all went into the ark,
Just to get out of the rain.

The animals went in four by four, hurrah,
   hurrah,

The animals went in four by four, hurrah,
  hurrah.
The animals went in four by four, the huge
  hippopotamus stuck in the door,
And they all went into the ark,
Just to get out of the rain.

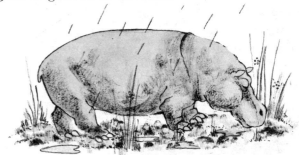

The animals went in five by five, hurrah,
  hurrah,
The animals went in five by five, hurrah,
  hurrah.
The animals went in five by five, by eating all
  day they kept alive,
And they all went into the ark,
Just to get out of the rain.

The animals went in six by six, hurrah, hurrah,
The animals went in six by six, hurrah, hurrah.
The animals went in six by six, the hyena
  laughed at the monkey's tricks,
And they all went into the ark,
Just to get out of the rain.
The animals went in seven by seven, hurrah,
  hurrah,

The animals went in seven by seven, hurrah,
  hurrah.
The animals went in seven, by seven, the little
  pig thought he was going to heaven,
And they all went into ark,
Just to get out of the rain.

The animals went in eight by eight, hurrah
  hurrah,
The animals went in eight by eight, hurrah,
  hurrah.
The animals went in eight by eight, they
  hurried and hustled because it was late,
And they all went into the ark,
Just to get out of the rain.

The animals went in nine by nine, hurrah,
  hurrah,
The animals went in nine by nine, hurrah,
  hurrah.
The animals went in nine by nine,
Old Noah shouted out, "Cut that line",
And they all went into the ark,
Just to get out of the rain.

The animals went in ten by ten, hurrah,
  hurrah,
The animals went in ten by ten, hurrah,
  hurrah.
The animals went in ten by ten, if you like
  this song you can sing it again,
And they all went into the ark,
Just to get out of the rain.

125   She Sells Seashells
She sells seashells on the sad seashore.

126   Peter Piper
Peter Piper picked a peck of pickled pepper.
A peck of pickled pepper, Peter Piper picked.
If Peter Piper picked a peck of pickled pepper,
Where's the peck of pickled pepper, Peter Piper
    picked?

127*   Thirty Days Has September   (A)
Thirty days has September,
April, June and November.
All the rest have thirty-one
Excepting February alone,
Which has but 28 days clear
And 29 in each leap year.

128*   The King's Breakfast   (G)
The King asked the Queen, and
The Queen asked the Dairymaid,
"Could we have some butter for
The Royal slice of bread?"
The Queen asked the Dairymaid,
The Dairymaid said: "Certainly,
I'll go and tell the cow, now
Before she goes to bed."
The Dairymaid she curtsied,
And went and told the Alderney:
"Don't forget the butter for
The Royal slice of bread."
The Alderney said sleepily:
"You'd better tell His Majesty
That many people nowadays
Like marmalade instead."
The Dairymaid said: "Fancy!"
And went to Her Majesty.

She curtsied to the Queen, and
She turned a little red.
"Excuse me, Your Majesty,
For taking of the liberty,
But marmalade is tasty if
It's very thickly spread."
The Queen said: "Oh!"
And went to His Majesty.
"Talking of the butter for
The Royal slice of bread,
Many people think that
Marmalade is nicer,
Would you like to try a little
Marmalade instead?"
The King said: "Bother!",
And then he said: "Oh deary me."
The King sobbed: "Oh deary me,"
And went back to bed.

"Nobody," he whimpered,
"Could call me a fussy man.
I *only* want a little bit
Of butter for my bread."
The Queen said: "There, there,"
And went to the Dairymaid.
The Dairymaid said: "There, there,"
And went to the shed.
The cow said "There, there,
I didn't really mean it,
Here's milk for his porringer
And butter for his bread."
The Queen took the butter
And brought it to His Majesty.
The king said: "Butter—eh?"
And bounced out of bed.
"Nobody," he said,
As he kissed her tenderly,
"Nobody," he said,
As he slid down the bannisters,
"Nobody, my darling,
Could call me a fussy man,
But I do like a little bit of butter for my bread."

130* There Was An Old Woman Who Swallowed A Fly (A)

There was an old woman who swallowed a fly.
I wonder why she swallowed a fly.
Poor old woman, she's bound to die.

There was an old woman who swallowed a
    spider
That wriggled and wriggled and wriggled inside
    her.
She swallowed the spider to catch the fly.
I wonder why she swallowed a fly.
Poor old woman, she's bound to die.

There was an old woman who swallowed a bird.
How absurd to swallow a bird!
She swallowed the bird to catch the spider,
That wriggled and wriggled and wriggled inside
    her.
She swallowed the spider to catch the fly.
I wonder why she swallowed a fly.
Poor old woman, she's bound to die.

129 My Aunt She Died A Month Ago (C)

My aunt, she died a month ago
And left me all her riches,
A feather bed and a wooden leg,
And a pair of calico breeches,
A coffee pot without a spout,
A cup without a handle,
A tobacco box without a lid,
And half a penny candle.

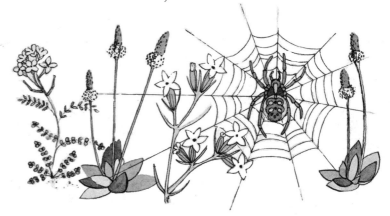

There was an old woman who swallowed a cat,
Fancy that! She swallowed a cat!
She swallowed the cat to catch the bird.
How absurd to swallow a bird!
She swallowed the bird to catch the spider,
That wriggled and wriggled and wriggled
    inside her.
She swallowed the spider to catch the fly.
I wonder why she swallowed a fly.
Poor old woman, she's bound to die.

There was an old woman who swallowed a dog.
She went the whole hog and swallowed a dog.
She swallowed the dog to catch the cat.
Fancy that! She swallowed a cat!
She swallowed the cat to catch the bird.
How absurd to swallow a bird!
She swallowed the bird to catch the spider
That wriggled and wriggled and wriggled inside
    her.
She swallowed the spider to catch the fly.

I wonder why she swallowed a fly.
Poor old woman, she's bound to die.

There was an old woman who swallowed a cow.
I wonder how she swallowed a cow.
She swallowed the cow to catch the dog.
She went the whole hog and swallowed the dog.
She swallowed the dog to catch the cat.
Fancy that! She swallowed a cat!
She swallowed the cat to catch the bird.
How absurd to swallow a bird!
She swallowed the bird to catch the spider
That wriggled and wriggled and wriggled inside
    her.
She swallowed the spider to catch the fly.
I wonder why she swallowed a fly.
Poor old woman, she's bound to die.

There was an old woman who swallowed a
    horse.
She died, of course.

131*   **Spring Is Showery**   **(A)**

Spring is showery, flowery, bowery,
Summer is hoppy, croppy, poppy,
Autumn: slippy, drippy, nippy,
Winter: breezy, sneezy, freezy.

132*   **Ten Green Speckled Frogs**

Ten green speckled frogs
Sat on a speckled log,
Eating a most delicious bug.
Yum Yum.
One jumped into the pool
Where it was nice and cool.
Then there were nine green speckled frogs.
Glug Glug.

Nine green speckled frogs
Sat on a speckled log,
Eating a most delicious bug.
Yum Yum.
One jumped into the pool
Where it was nice and cool.
Then there were eight green speckled frogs.
Glug Glug.

Eight green speckled frogs, etc.

133   **The Owl And The Pussy Cat**   **(C)**

The owl and the pussy cat went to sea
In a beautiful pea green boat.
They took some honey and plenty of money
Wrapped up in a five pound note.
The owl looked up at the stars above
And sang to a small guitar,
"O lovely Pussy, O Pussy my love,
What a beautiful pussy you are!
   You are!
What a beautiful Pussy you are!"

Puss said to the owl, "You elegant fowl,
How charmingly sweet you sing.

O let us be married! Too long have we tarried,
But what shall we do for a ring?"
They sailed away for a year and a day
To the land where the Bong-tree grows,
And there in a wood a Piggy-wig stood
With a ring at the end of his nose,
    His nose,
    His nose,
With a ring at the end of his nose.

"Dear Pig, are you willing to sell for one shilling
Your ring?" Said the Piggy, "I will."
So they took it away, and were married next day
By the Turkey who lived on the hill.
They dined on mince, and slices of quince,
Which they ate with a runcible spoon.
And hand in hand on the edge of the sand
They danced by the light of the moon,
    The moon,
    The moon,
They danced by the light of the moon.

134 Who Has Seen The Wind   (E)

Who has seen the wind?
Neither I nor you.
But when the leaves hang trembling
The wind is passing through.
Who has seen the wind?
Neither you nor I.
But when the trees bow down their heads
The wind is passing by.

135 Whenever The Moon And Stars Are Set   (C)

Whenever the moon and stars are set,
Whenever the wind is high,
All night long in the dark and wet
A man goes riding by.
Late in the night when the fires are out,
Why does he gallop and gallop about?

Whenever the trees are crying aloud
And ships are tossed at sea,
By, on the highway, low and loud,
By, at the gallop goes he.
By, at the gallop he goes and then
By, he comes back at the gallop again.

INDEX OF TITLES OR FIRST LINES